Vermont Afternoons
with
ROBERT FROST

Vermont Afternoons

with

ROBERT FROST

by Vrest Orton

Alan C. Hood & Company, Inc.
CHAMBERSBURG, PENNSYLVANIA

ISBN 0-911469-18-4

Published by Alan C. Hood & Co., Inc.
Chambersburg, PA 17201

Copies of *Vermont afternoons with Robert Frost*
may be obtained by sending $13.50 per copy to:

Alan C. Hood & Co., Inc.
P.O. Box 775, Chambersburg, PA 17201

Price includes postage and handling.

Quantity discounts are available to
dealers and non-profit organizations.

Write on letterhead for details.

Library of Congress Cataloging-in-Publication Data

Orton, Vrest, 1897-
    Vermont afternoons with Robert Frost / by Vrest Orton.
      p. cm.
    ISBN 0-911469-18-4
      1. Frost, Robert, 1874-1963--Poetry. 2. Poets, American--
Poetry. 3. Vermont--Poetry. I.Title.

PS3565.R8 V4 2000
811'.54--dc21

                                        00-035102

          10 9 8 7 6 5 4 3 2 1

To my three sons

Geoffrey, Lyman, and Jeremy

❦❦ TABLE OF CONTENTS ❦❦

Wood engravings by Thomas Bewick.

🌿 FOREWORD 🌿

I

There are few perfect moments in a man's life. One is when he sees genius plain. Millions now living will die and never know this ecstatic pause in eternity because there is, of course, not always a genius in every lifetime; more often there are none in several.

One defines genius by the kind of gift it gives to posterity. To have received two such perfect gifts in one lifetime is not a matter of choice. It is only by the grace of God that I have heard Artur Rubinstein play Chopin, and Robert Frost talk.

In the presence of genius the world falls away and a human being is one with the cosmos. The privilege of being moved by Rubinstein and by Frost into perfect grace is too rare and unique an experience to bear examination, or to explain.

One does not sit and hear Rubinstein play or Frost talk. *Hear* is too prosaic a word to describe some kind of assimulation into the inner recesses of the heart. A man who has been lucky enough to embrace such magic will never be the same again. He no longer exists, he lives.

I began to assimilate Robert Frost's conversation and verse forty years ago; I have never been the same since.

II

Vermont Afternoons with Robert Frost is a tribute I want to pay to a friendship. In some friendships the colors fade. Not in this one. Phyllis McGinley, in her charming book, *Saint Watching,* describes it perfectly when she writes that "it restores the spirit to learn that there can be friendships where nothing is asked and everything given."

During the decade of the 1920s Frost was living in the stone house on Route 7 in South Shaftsbury, Vermont. Later, about 1930, he gave that to his son Carol and moved to "The Gully," a small one-storey Vermont farmhouse a mile or so on a back road east of the village. I formed the habit from 1930 on of going to visit with him, hoping I'd not wear out his generosity if I stopped an hour. These memorable visits did not stop in one hour. They usually went on all the afternoon; sometimes into the evening and once in a while all night. Frost would also come over to visit at my house, but most of these sessions took place at his. His generosity was inexhaustible.

I suppose it may be said that those were afternoons I did not spend . . . I saved them up.

III

One afternoon we were talking about what makes poets poets. Frost said, "What you say isn't yours." And then he quickly added, "A poet can brag only about form."

Of course he said it better in his well-known lines:

> *Let chaos storm!*
> *Let cloud shapes swarm!*
> *I wait for form.*

To me, over thirty-five years ago, that was a profound remark. I never dreamed that the day would come when I should enjoy the proof of it. It was a long wait!

But the day came, or rather the night.

It was like this: about the year 1960, I'd suddenly awake, out of a sound sleep, at three o'clock in the morning. In that strange, eerie and uncanny interlude between consciousness and sleep, some of the conversation I'd enjoyed with Robert Frost thirty years before seemed to be striving for expression. It was not exactly a dream nor exactly a memory. I can't explain it very well because sometimes only a few words would emerge crystal clear out of the mind. Sometimes two or three sentences . . . never more. But always enough to make sharp sense and to evoke vividly a perfect recall of those days when every sentence Robert Frost uttered was to me heavy with meaning, wisdom, and light. So lucid were these moments that I'd come wide awake, take up a pencil and write exactly the words the subconscious had given up.

These thrilling and exultant moments in the nighttime went on for a few weeks and resulted in pages of notes. Then the door to that deep well closed and was never opened again.

It would have been rewarding enough if I'd kept only the notes. But in some mysterious fashion I felt compelled to write out, the next day or two, some sort of extension of what the night notes had evoked.

This is where this volume comes from.

The ideas are Robert Frost's.* After something, I know not what, had triggered the subconscious mind and made it give up Frost, I managed in my own amateur fashion, to translate what came out into a form that seemed to be, as I remembered it, the way Robert Frost would have wanted the ideas expressed.

The reader, at this point, will probably reach the logical conclusion that the verse in this book is a contrived attempt, even if a poor one at best, to imitate Robert Frost's poetry. He would be wrong.

Anyone who understands the greatness of Frost's work, and who knew the man, would never in God's world be presumptuous, to say nothing of damned fool enough, to think that any mortal man could imitate Frost.

* This applies to all the verse in this book with the exception of *Drinking Fountains* which Frost told on himself and which I also heard from a Middlebury resident.

The ideas were told to me by Robert Frost. The form is mine. If the form in which one word follows another seems natural and right but sounds like Frost, I can't help it. The form sprang naturally from the Frost substance.

Perhaps one can blame the whole thing on the spirit of the Poetic Muse which hovers just a little above our heads and makes fools of most of us. But once in a while, in a century or so, the same muse makes a poet like Robert Frost.

To call what follows poetry is to draw an extremely odious comparison that won't stand the light of day. One who criticizes what follows because it is not poetry, can't stand the light of logic.

At this point it would be appropriate to quote Bulwer Lytton who remarked that, "Genius does what it must, and talent does what it can."

IV

After the stock market crash in 1929, when I was living in New York and seeing Frost once in a while, he precipitated a decision one day by asking me, in his inimitable fashion, why I didn't "ease off on New York." He declared that what you are escaping *to* is more important than what you are escaping *from*. I had first met him in the mid-twenties when H. L. Mencken introduced us. But meeting people is not, however, a friendship. My friendship with Robert Frost began when I left New York briefly, in 1930, to try out Vermont. That brief trial resulted, years later, in a total conviction of me. Vermont has held me firmly in bondage ever since.

But in 1930 it was time to go. George Jean Nathan had quit and even H. L. Mencken himself was figuring on returning to Baltimore to leave the *American Mercury* in other hands. An even greater calamity was soon to cast a pall over the nation.

It was, as I recall, in 1929 that Frost had purchased the Vermont farmhouse called "The Gully" and, in one of our chance meetings which were few up to this time, he asked me to come and see him if I did "ease off on New York."

Thus it came about that my afternoons with Robert Frost began and, I am thankful to say, continued though less frequently after the thirties, up to the late fifties. It was in these later years that I began to enjoy another side of Robert Frost. I had been fortunate enough to know most of the leading American authors and early had become convinced that Robert Frost possessed a unique distinction: he was as great a man as he was a poet. Now to my delight there was revealed a new facet of his personality.

He was, I had soon found out, a Democrat. From that tag, most people assumed, glibly, of course, that he was a New Dealer and later an ardent marcher in the ranks of the New Frontier. Nothing could be further from the truth. The kind of old-fashioned Democrat by principle that Robert Frost professed to be exists in lesser numbers these days. As it will be shown in one of his letters, Frost was far from being a liberal and was constantly pained by the mess the libertarians were, he surmised, about to make of the world. In fact, being the wise man that he was, he sensed the future before any of us. By 1940, he could say, and say it in his usual charming, if prophetic, vision, that Eleanor Roosevelt* was "trying to homogenize American society, so that the cream would never rise to the top again." He was fond of repeating this phrase.

It also tickled me to read his reaction to the "new literature" that began to rise like flotsam in the thirties when Marx was the father, Freud the mother, and Russia the heaven to be striven for. Frost declared that these writers were producing "huge, shapeless gobs of raw sincerity, bellowing with pain."

Coming down to a much later period after Frost had left Shaftsbury, Vermont, and moved to a farm in the woods near Middlebury where he enlightened the annual sessions of the Bread Loaf Writers Conference, politics piqued his interest again. In session assembled, the honorable General Assembly of Vermont passed a resolution making Robert Frost poet laureate of the Green Mountain State. I never heard all that he said about this, but he did remark something to the effect that the air was too rarified on Olympus and the view from the top was sure to be obscured by the clouds.

To draw the conclusion that Robert Frost failed to

* Wife of President Franklin Delano Roosevelt.

appreciate the sincere honor, or that he was making fun of Vermonters, is wholly to misunderstand and miss the Frost brand of humor; or the Vermont brand. For by this time Frost had become so much of a Vermonter that it showed, both in his talk and his poetry.

I wondered, however, what he said years earlier when a famous political figure and a Vermonter referred to Frost in a public statement. Once when Calvin Coolidge was governor of Massachusetts and was being interviewed by the press, a reporter unable to think of a question apropos to the hour, asked the governor if he knew Robert Frost, "the poet."

To which Mr. Coolidge replied: "Oh, you mean that poet who has been hanging around the Statehouse?"

To imagine Robert Frost ever, in his life, "hanging around the Statehouse" is as wide a miss as the point of the governor's quip: the Vermont comic sense of both Robert Frost and Calvin Coolidge had come together and was one.

It's too bad that Robert Frost and Calvin Coolidge could not have known each other better ... neither was a waster of words.*

V

This, however, is not to be a biography of Robert

* Mr. Orton is also author of a book about Calvin Coolidge entitled, *Calvin Coolidge's Unique Vermont Inauguration,* published by The Calvin Coolidge Memorial Foundation, Inc., of Plymouth, Vermont.

Frost. It would be preposterous for me to attempt to explain him. To me, he and his work were there to enjoy, never to judge. I took him as he was. To the learned doctors of psychiatry and the psychic sciences I leave that profound task and, believe me they have embarked upon it. I enjoyed, never dissected.

But there are pages already in print revealing why Robert Frost did something a certain way, for example, when he was thirty-six, because somebody had scared him when he was six! If you like this kind of probing, you are welcome to it. I would as soon try to slice up Robert Frost in laboratory sections and analyze the specimens, as I would scrape the paint off a Rubens to see how they made pigments in those days!

Just to get down in print, somehow, the sparks that were struck off and by the grace of God came back to me in the nighttime, thirty odd years later, is, I think, something that Robert would just as lief I'd do as to ape some of the literary critics who now blithely and hurriedly explain everything Robert Frost was and everything his poetry meant. Oftentimes they are able to reveal meanings which, I know very well, would be new and surprising to Robert Frost himself were he alive this day.

One fall when I was visiting him in Cambridge, Massachusetts, he quipped that you can't pin a bard down like a dead butterfly. This was clearly a bit of anticipatory wisdom that explains the futility of contemporary socio-economic critics who, while they may profess some slight knowledge in that field, never knew Robert Frost and had no notion whatsoever of what he was talking about either as a talker or a poet. A doctor's degree in political science or psychology, or any other subject, earned and performed within the confines of Manhattan, Chicago, or Los Angeles, hardly ever prepares a man to know a stone wall, or to understand Robert Frost.

The greatness of Robert Frost transcends American poetry. It is the greatness of Western Civilization.

Someday, all the critics will know.

Someday they will sicken of the touchstones of Freud and Marx, abandon dead-end rationality, give up the futility of dialectics, and open their hearts . . . if they have any. Then, perhaps a century hence, if their ilk has not destroyed the world, they will know that the annals of American poetry of this age will then exist, principally, as a footnote to Robert Frost and his work.

VI

In between visits, and for long spells when we did not see each other often, letters went back and forth. During Robert Frost's lifetime, none was published. But as I read these again, after almost forty years, many revealing passages seem to have bearing on his character. From these I quote a few paragraphs.

In 1930, I had written and published *Proceedings of the Company of Amateur Brewers,* a book on how to make beer in the home. Since, during Prohibition, it was illegal to publish recipes on how to make intoxicating beverages, this book was given free to members of a group called the "Company of Amateur Brewers." Frost made some comment from time to time on this subject and especially in a letter of September, 1930, from Shaftsbury, Vermont:

"I wish you were where you could drop in off-hand when you felt forlorn. The wine I couldn't provide. I don't know how to make it and it takes too much time and trouble now to buy it. And it seems more rebellious than luxurious or genial to sit drinking it in any company however good. I can't stay roused up enough to talk and act rebellious in my pleasures. Pleasures and rebellion don't mix with me. Stolen sweets are another matter. They are an individual thing. This struggle for drink is a mass movement. I could supply some talk. I like talk the same as you do . . ."

In that same year I had edited a kind of Vermont annual encyclopedia, known since 1802 as *Walton's Register*. For 1930, it was changed in title to *The Vermont Year Book & Guide* and for the first time, each of the 248 townships carried a brief note outlining the history, as well as some geographical and biographical data. To this book Frost often referred:

"Sometime in the fall when the flood of summer people has subsided, you and I will be left still clinging to the rocks of Vermont. Then we can see each other. But if I haven't seen you, I have thought of you and read you. Of course, your twilight passage in *The Colophon* pleased me. So also your *Vermont Year Book & Guide* in which I have read every single town once and some towns twice. From now on it will be easier for me to masquerade as a Vermonter. Next year put in more elevations. Nothing is so uplifting as the heights of small towns. The height of Peacham did me good. I knew the height of Danby and Peru. I want to know more. A book like that enriched year by year could become the most interesting book of the age . . ."

The Vermont Year Book & Guide, alas, did not live up to Frost's prophecy and become "the most interesting book of the age." I had been asked to edit this Vermont compendium by Charles Tuttle, a very old friend and father of my present publisher. Unfortunately, the book fell into other hands in spite of Mr. Tuttle's enthusiasm for the new format, and the historical notes and other data which Frost apparently enjoyed were abandoned. Although Frost does not dwell at this point, in the letter above, he told me on one of our visits that he wished to find another town in Vermont that would suit his hay fever better than South Shaftsbury. In August, 1930, he again spoke of this:

> "The small town is as bad in its way as the big city. I for my part never said it wasn't. Something you want to do and the chance to do it is all that makes any place endurable. Every little while when I am out of work I have a slump about where I live and look around the ground and up at the sky for a refuge. It was in such a mood that I read your *Year Book*. I considered every town in it as a possible escape from Shaftsbury . . . I'm off here for hay fever. I shall be home by September 21st."

For a brief time, I had rented a house in a Vermont country village and, since it had been the residence of a former clergyman, it became to me "The Parsonage." Frost later wrote from Amherst:

> "Just a word to tell you that it was as much fun as finding The Parsonage on the Common myself as to hear the story of your finding it. I am going to live in a place like that before I get through. I shall want to have a good look at it as soon as possible. You see where I am now. I've just arrived for my three months in residence without duties. I classify in the census at this time of year as one of the gainfully unemployed

[21]

. . . Amherst is a pleasant little town and our street is almost as quiet as yours . . . I can't come to prove that right away but I'll tell you what I can do. I can put a brand new book of mine into your house as a hostage . . . if you'll let me . . ."

In 1929, I had founded, in New York City, *The Colophon,* a book collector's magazine, and was on the editorial board. I was then compiling bibliographies of American authors for a book on American first editions. To this magazine Frost refers when, on December 13, 1930, he writes:

". . . I'm up to my eyes in Amherst. I am immersed in Amherst for another month or so now. I have no classes I can call my own. But I go a visiting on other people's classes. And the result may not be better educated boys, but it means an exhausted me. I don't have to do anything. I do it for the fun of it. So don't be sorry for me. Several of the boys are sorry for certain omissions in *The Colophon* bibliography. We must tend to those in yours . . ."

In 1929 when we were planning *The Colophon,* Frederic Melcher, editor of *The Publishers Weekly,* was preparing a bibliographic article of the first editions of Robert Frost which appeared in one of the first issues.

Since no bibliography was ever perfectly complete, I assume Frost was referring in his last sentence to the opportunity of suggesting *errata* and *addenda* to my work then being prepared for book publication.

This letter was followed almost immediately by another, dated December 28, 1930, from Baltimore:

> "We are in Baltimore with a daughter sick in the hospital for Christmas and the future a blank uncertainty. I should like to have you go ahead on the book if you can see the way. My firsts are all in a box at my son Carol's house in South Shaftsbury where you could see them or get them to take home with you, just as you pleased. I know you'd be more careful of them than I ever would, particularly of the first . . . I may have to make an expedition west to place Marjorie somewhere for her lungs. I shan't be able to stay with her now but think of spending part of the year with her later. I sound fairly confused. Marjorie has been poorly for several years. This tubercular threat is new. We are a good deal upset . . ."

On July 25, 1931, he wrote from Evergreen, Colorado:

> ". . . I've been thinking of you lately and wondering what you were thinking of me for

having neglected you so long. You must not think too hardly and you won't when you hear my excuses. We have had one sickness on top of another ever since last Christmas. You knew we had to be in Baltimore on account of my daughter Marjorie much of the winter. In the end we brought her to Boulder, Colorado. We had scarcely wound up at Amherst when we discovered that my son Carol's wife was sick of the same sickness and would have to be taken away from the New England climate. Carol was busy selling out his farm business the two or three weeks we were in South Shaftsbury. That isn't all the story. We were four weeks at Montauk, Long Island, with my daughter Lesley who had a serious time with having a second child. So you see without having to be told in exclamations. We are out here giving Marjorie a brief vacation from her sanitarium. She'll go back to it and then we'll go east soon. But all is obscure ahead. I may not get settled down in South Shaftsbury before the middle of September after the first frosts have knocked the hay fever. When I do I shall want to see you and hear all about your new publishing. I owe you a book, don't I? I notice you are advertising several books about Vermont and have meant to have at least one of them. I seem to have too much to think of for decency. This is a beautiful country. But hot where we sojourn thirty miles west of Denver, up Bear Canyon under Mt. Evans of nearly 14,000 feet. There's snow in sight. Every two or three hours the drought is broken with a bump of thunder but no rain. The region is flowery. I am learning to like the U.S. section by section . . ."

In 1931, I had founded a book publishing venture which undertook to issue Vermont books, the most notable being a four-volume compilation of Vermont material entitled *The Green Mountain Series*. During this period, I spent considerable time with Sinclair Lewis at his house in Barnard, Vermont, and also in journeys around Vermont. Lewis became incensed, at one point, when *The Nation* reviewed *The Green Mountain Series* and, as was (and still is) its wont, sneered at anything that smacked of American ideals and ancient wisdom. Lewis wrote a slashing attack on *The Nation* and its senseless diatribe against Vermont. This I published in a broadside on September 16, 1931, in an edition limited to 375 copies. It was to this that Frost refers in the following letter of October 23, 1931. I should say that I disposed of my interests in this country publishing venture in 1932 and returned to New York:

". . . Come over someday soon and have lunch with us. It will be fine to hear from you all about your new books . . . Bully for Lewis. That's the way to talk to them liberals. They howl at the injustices of this country and then seize the first opportunity to commit injustice themselves. I hope Lewis convicted them. Good on his head. I suppose he makes a mistake in assuming they want the nation de-urbanized. They, the likes of them, are all for having it industrialized, centralized, de-individualized and sovietized under a Stalin or other son-of-a Marx. But never mind. *The Nation* heard itself *characterized*. I may be a radical and long for revolution, but I shall have to choose the kind of revolution . . ."

On November 21, 1931, Frost wrote from South Shaftsbury:

"You don't come over the mountain, and we're sorry. You must be busy and we're glad. We hear of that press of yours on every hand . . . Now we're going away for a week or so to settle businesses and by the time we get back snow may have closed the pass for pleasure driving. In that case consider our invitation commuted to one on us at Amherst during our three months in residence there . . . I want to see you. There are several things I wanted to talk with you about."

One could go on quoting more Frost letters but the foregoing seem a proper sample of his thought and his own way of expressing it. As the years went on, the letters were fewer because we exchanged ideas more by visits and chance meetings. I remember once meeting Frost on a Rutland Railroad train: he was going north to Middlebury and I was coming home from Washington. We had a good visit. It was one of the last visits we had together. He came to Weston last in 1955 and left me the magnificent portrait by Clara Sipprell. I saw him only a couple times after that.

Robert Frost lived to be 88 years old but his life for those who enjoyed his friendship was too short.

Weston, Vermont   VREST ORTON

Robert Frost to Vrest Orton "in lasting friendship."
Clara Sipprell photograph.

Standing in the wind and sun
one day on a hillside
in Vermont,
        Robert Frost

*"Shouting in the wind to Vrest Orton
on a hillside in Vermont."*

Robert Frost and Vrest Orton at Frost's farm in Vermont.

Robert Frost and Vrest Orton on stoop of Frost's farm.

❧ THE POEMS ❧

What Else Had Failed

I

Hardly a man comes up this far
Without asking me the same question:
How can I live so far away!
Since you didn't pose the question,
You'll be the first to have my answer.

II

I came up here to see how man had failed!
Down country he seems to have won all his wars;
He's littered land and befouled water.
He's a stranger to peace and the clean heart.
The fear of God is not in him.
Up here, I thought, maybe someone else
Might have the upper hand.

III

Just a minute, Robert. You know the Bible says
. . . The Lord put Man in the Garden of Eden
To dress it and keep it.
Do you think he's done well in Vermont?

IV

I don't know as he's had a chance.
But I'll let you in on something . . .
I wanted to get back far enough
To learn what else had failed.

After His Kind

I

Wait a minute while I read *you* something!
Last time you quoted the Bible . . .
Now I'll quote a little to you;
I'll start at the beginning.

II

"God said let the earth
Bring forth the fruit tree yielding fruit . . .
After his kind,
Whose seed was in itself,
After his kind.
And God said let the earth bring forth
The living creature,
After his kind.
And cattle and creeping thing,
And beast of the earth,
After his kind . . .
And it was so."

III

I had the audacity to interrupt:
That's great poetry!

[36]

IV

Of course it is . . . but you missed the point;
It's great sense.
I'd like to drive it way through the thick skulls
Of today's egalitarians,
Who are fixing things in America
So cream will never rise to the top again.

A Beaker of Sunlight

I

We were standing in the barn between the two mows.
It wasn't quite spring yet. If it had been
You would have kept the barn door open
To let the sun in.
As it was, the sun came in in spite of the door;
It leaked through a slathole in the roof
Where some shingle forgot to overlap.
And stood a slim shaft of dusty light on the floor.
The boards were wide, worn and knarled:
Each knot was raised a little, like a hill
And all the valleys were soft with hayseed and
    spilled grain.

II

You said something about how a knot
Will survive, like character in a man's face.
The knot being the harder part of the board . . .
The face being the softer part of the man.
I looked at your face.
The wisdom and the troubles of the world
Were stamped upon it.
But the wisdom, like the knots,
Was what made the configuration.

III

We took seats there on open sacks of grain
Half used, with the tops rolled down.
Mine was provender and yours oats.

> *When I was a boy, I used to eat provender by the*
> *fistful.*

You smiled; *why don't you do it now?*
Then we'll walk over to the trough
And have a drink of my good spring water.

IV

As you handed me the tin cup full of water
Another shaft revealed a round silver mirror
And sprinkled its bright surface with the same dust.
I didn't hesitate before I tipped the cup
But I think you expected me to.
I quoted you:

> *Such was life in the Golden Gate:*
> *Gold dusted all we drank and ate,*
> *And I was one of the children told,*
> *'We all must eat our peck of gold'.*

V

You laughed. *You have me there,* you said.
But to quote a man back is no fair.
The habit will bring you your share of troubles.

[39]

VI

What I was going to say, though, was this;
I never saw a man down a beaker of sunlight
Without blowing off the bubbles!

In the Orchard

I

We sat talking in front of your fireplace, I remember,
All that September afternoon. The air was nippy
But the talk had warmed me; I don't know about
    you.
I saw, but didn't think about the cold ashes from
    another fire.
You did.
Better get some wood, you said, standing.

II

   I'll help.

I followed you through the kitchen and out the
    back door.
Dusk had fallen, the inanimate grass was bleak, the
    apple trees forlorn:
More spidery silhouettes than trees, hugging
    the gentle slope
Back of the house. Guarding something, you had
    remarked archly,
But never finished the thought . . .
The wood pile got in the way.

III

You prized, I remember, a sharp axe as you prized
    all sharp tools,
Like words. This time you used the axe.
Let me do it, I said . . . moving toward the chopping
    block . . .
A futile gesture.
I like to chop wood, you retorted to the tune
    of the neat quick split
That opened cleanly the true grain of the maple.
You can't do anything, you added (to soften
    the retort),
With a man who likes to chop wood!

IV

As I stood waiting, bewitched by your skill,
My eyes lifted over you and the low dark woodpile
Into the darkening apple orchard . . .
Guarding something, you had suggested. This time
    it was a lad
Stretched out, back to trunk, with notebook, or
    something white
In his hand.
Pretty late to be reading, or writing, I remember
    thinking, not saying;
Maybe he's sleeping.

V

Who's that, was what I blurted out.

VI

Mark's boy, you answered, never missing a stroke
   of the axe.
He's visiting here a spell.
Taller than his father. You'd see . . . if he'd stand.
But he didn't stand.
Lazy, I thought, but kept that one to myself.

   Robert, what's the matter with him chopping
   The wood on this place?

VII

He don't chop wood, you said in mock Vermont
   venacular,
Keeping your eyes on the chore at hand and almost
   matching
Each word to the neat cleaving of the fatal axe.
He's a poet.

Learn to Follow

I

I don't want to do much plowing any more.
But years back, in New Hampshire,
I did more plowing than I wanted to,
Or, as things turned out,
Than was needed.

II

Both my State of New Hampshire
And your State of Vermont
Have one thing in common . . .
You can't plow a deep furrow.
Stones are harder than the plow-share.
We both rout out a lot of stones
And tug'm by stone-boat to make a wall . . .
But this ain't exactly the purpose of plowing.

III

Purpose of plowing, I said,
is to plant.
That's not it, at all!
The purpose of plowing is to learn
To follow, to follow.

IV

Or to plow a straight furrow,
I ventured.

That's not it at all!
You've got to learn how to follow.
When you're behind a walking plow,
A root can throw you, one way or 't'other,
A boulder can wedge you out of line,
And spoil your temper, and the plow's.
You'd be a damned poor farmer,
If you allowed these diversions to prevent
Plowing a straight furrow.
The horse knows where he's going . . .
You'd better learn to follow . . . to follow!

V

I see your point . . . it's a philosophical one.

Nothing to do with philosophy!
Just plain common sense.
I learned a long time ago
To do a little following of wise men,
Before I commenced handing out any wisdom of
  my own.

VI

That's why I'm here, I rejoined.

Oh, come on! I deserved that!
If Ezra Pound were here, he'd cry *touché*.
But you know, I'll tell you a state secret:
I got all-fired tired of hearing that word!

[45]

What Kind of a Dog

I

I'm going to walk the dog down
Through the pasture to the brook,
Where I keep a trout in a pool, by the wall . . .
Or the pool keeps the trout. I never know which
Keeps which.
Better come along.

II

What kind of a dog, indeed!
If you'll go with us down to the pool
I won't ask what kind of a man you are.
If you won't ask who's walking whom!
I'm not sure whether the dog wanted to go down
     there first,
Or I did.
But we can all go together,
If you don't ask too many questions.

III

Now about this word *Keeping*.
The fellow down the road, he keeps sheep.

Bronson, down to the four corners, keeps, I presume,
    cows.
Some men keep horses, ducks, geese or mules;
I knew a man once who kept a bear.
In my time I've been guilty of even keeping
    hens . . .
The dumbest of all living creatures!
Yet they produce, without benefit of man,
The most perfect shape on earth . . .
I wonder if they know!

IV

But come along.
If you'd just as lief lift that bottom wire;
I'd rather crawl under than fall over.

V

Why do I keep this dog?
You ask one of the three greatest questions.
(None has a proper answer.)
What is love?
Where are we going?
That's the other two.

VI

There is, though, a sort of a retort
To your question . . .
I'm not offering it as an answer:—
But I don't *keep* this dog!

[47]

VII

Look at him . . . almost down there now.
(Yes . . . yes . . . we'll be along, if you wouldn't
    hurry so.)
The damned animal . . . always running way ahead,
Then looking back and grinning:
A bone would melt in his mouth!

VIII

No, I don't keep him.
He keeps me.

Another Farm over Back

I

*Robert, they tell me you bought another farm, over
    back.*
What are you planning . . . to farm it?

No . . . I'd hate to think I was reduced to that.
They auctioned the place off, not many there;
I took it because nobody else bid.
It's lonely, hard to get to or from,
And the barn roof has fallen in.

II

Looks like a poor bargain to me.
You can make more money making stories.

That's the whole point; I got a story.
It came with the place.
Let me tell you:
Right after the auction, a little runt came up to me;
Wanted to know if I aimed to farm it. Like you.
(Everybody wants to get me back to farming,
    seems if.)
Said if I didn't, he'd kind of like to get some things
    out of my barn.
Wanted to know what I was asking for the drinking
    fountains,
Said they were built into the stanchions.

[49]

III

I suppose you gave them away.
You're always too generous.

No. I fooled you that time. I said to the fellow,
His name, I believe, was and mostly likely is,
    Mead . . .
If he hasn't starved himself to death by penury.
I said to him:—tell you what, Mr. Mead, I don't
    aim to farm it.
You go in there and take out the fountains . . .
Make up your mind what they're worth to you,
Then you pay me just half that amount.

IV

That seems pretty fair to me.
What did he say?

Well, he said, is that what you're asking, and I said,
That *is* what I am asking.
I have no need for drinking fountains. You take
    them.

V

What happened?
Nothing.
Not then. But a year later, Mead came around.
It was, in fact, last spring. He stood about where
    you're standing now;

Overalls hitched up tight to tuck neatly into his
    rubber boots . . .
A little runt, not over five feet and bald as a beet.
He stood there, scuffing one boot back and forth
    in the mud like a horse,
While he balanced on the other.
I waited.
If a man has got something to say,
I don't interrupt him.

VI

"Well," he hemmed for a spell . . . then he blurted
    out:
"Mister, seeing you don't aim to farm the place,
I don't know but if I might buy them drinking
    fountains."
Then he looked down sheepishly at the mud hole
    his boot was digging and added:
"But they're so all-fired old, and hard to get out . . .
I don't know how I can afford
To pay what you're asking."

White Flags in Winter

I

I would never live where I couldn't feel freedom,
I stay here but I live in Vermont:
You don't get off scot-free there with freedom;
They make you take the Freeman's Oath.

II

You've seen the farmwife hanging clothes on
    the porch:
She never frets how it looks to a passerby.
Freemen don't dwell on their freedom's showing.
She's more concerned if the wind is blowing
To do the drying before the freezing . . .
If the freezing gets the better of drying
She'll face another chore more trying.

III

Up the road to the Gully last fall
I saw washings out on porch lines.

IV

You will . . . you will! I call them white flags
    flying,
Not in surrender but freedom proclaiming.
You should never be surprised . . .
Vermonters know there are other prides more
    prized.

Immortal

I

There's no use saying we'll come again,
If you can't admit to original cause.
Man was not made for pleasure or pain,
He was made to illustrate flaws.

II

Don't tell me there's no purpose or reason,
If nothing is all.
What would be the sense of this season,
Or the color this fall?
Or the ripe apple on this tree,
Or you, or me, or that cow?

III

If there is a hereafter
There is a before now.

Vermont

Of course it's my state!
I don't know whether I adopted Vermont
Or Vermont adopted me . . .
Either way's good enough;
I'm rooted in.

One Life

I

Do I want to live a century?
I never measure life by length . . .
Better invent a gauge to measure depth.

II

The reason I brought up the question,
A man in our town is 103 years old today.

III

Had he done anything?

IV

Many men learn how to save up life
And fondle it with loving care,
Like a miser feeling both sides of every coin,
Or a mouse hiding the last remaining crumb.
The question is,
How has he spent it?

V

He hasn't said!

The Well

I

Up to now I never complained
About the ignorance of city men;
There are so many common things they don't
    know,
It would be easier to list what they do know!

II

Robert, you can't expect them
To be well versed in country things,
As you are . . . quoting you.

III

I don't . . . that would be asking too much
But I do expect a modicum of common sense,
Here and there!
The other day one wanted to pull up the well
    bucket
Before the rope went slack the second time.

Half a Poet

Emerson said he was only half a poet.
There's a fellow here in Vermont
Who writes newspaper verse:
He thinks I'm the other half.

On Your Melancholy Day

I

What's the use of taking on so!
Let me show you the back orchard.
Just step here to the door:—
See how the apple blossoms sprinkle the dusk,
As stars sprinkle the night.

II

Witness those pansies near the step . . .
They look up when you look down.
If you want to walk out I'll show you
How good the bark feels on the pines.
See the lilacs over there near the barn;
I call them Whitman's un-neglected flowers,
You can smell 'em from here.

III

If you want to take a step to the brook,
Live moss still embraces the stones,
And every pebble at the bottom of the brook
Is as clean as the running water.

IV

There's nothing so encouraging as a new blade of
    grass,
Or a fresh shoot of corn pushing out of the ground.
I'm not an optimist,
But I'm glad to offer you nature's consolations,
On your melancholy day.

Failure

I

I tell you it's important
To learn to fail . . .
One time or another.

II

It's sheer vanity to say so;
But just suppose I had not failed,
As a farmer.

The New Jungle

I

One Spring afternoon, standing by the front steps,
You spoke of Nature's constant success.
In spite of all the hazards,
She always puts forth a new green,
You said, looking toward the softness of the upland
     pasture,
And up beyond, to the woodlands where the sun
Spattered the tender leaves of the maple and the
     poplar.
Someday all this will be destroyed!

II

You mean in spite of all that man can do
Nature will take over . . .
The old law of the jungle?

III

I'm thinking of a new jungle . . .
And a different kind of nature.
The awesome ignorance of man
Is only equalled by his senseless greed.
The tyranny of greed and ignorance
Will be the law of the new jungle.

[61]

Blue Jays

I

Come over here and see my new bird house.
The hole the size of a dollar?
I took an augur.
Not to keep blue jays in
But big birds out.

II

Do many go in?

III

I don't know.
I'm a bird lover
Not a counter.

Not There

I

You'll doubtless find, somewhere in this mowing,
A leaf of green or a blooming flower,
That had just as soon tell where I'm going
And, just as glibly, predict the hour.

II

Someday I'll be buried, deep and sound:
They'd soon as know what they're blooming over,
As what-it-may-be that leaves the ground
Cares what may be there, under the clover.

III

They can prate and pray, and go on singing,
And bid farewell to trouble and care.
But while the bells in the steeple are ringing,
Whatever was down is no longer there.